Contents

A Lucky Find   5

Egyptian Adventure   41

The Travelling Players   77

The Flying Machine   113

OXFORD

UNIVERSITY PRESS

Authors and illustrators

A Lucky Find written by Roderick Hunt, illustrated by Alex Brychta

Egyptian Adventure written by Roderick Hunt, illustrated by Alex Brychta

The Travelling Players written by Roderick Hunt, illustrated by Nick Schon

The Flying Machine written by Roderick Hunt, illustrated by Alex Brychta

OXFORD
UNIVERSITY PRESS

Great Clarendon Street, Oxford, OX2 6DP, United Kingdom

Oxford University Press is a department of the University of Oxford. It furthers the University's objective of excellence in research, scholarship, and education by publishing worldwide. Oxford is a registered trade mark of Oxford University Press in the UK and in certain other countries

A Lucky Find, *Egyptian Adventure*, *The Travelling Players*, *The Flying Machine* text © Roderick Hunt 2001, 2015

A Lucky Find, *Egyptian Adventure*, *The Flying Machine* illustrations © Alex Brychta 2001, 2015
The Travelling Players illustrations by Nick Schon © Oxford University Press 2015

Egyptian Adventure, *The Flying Machine* first published in 2001
A Lucky Find, *The Travelling Players* first published in 2015

This Edition first published in 2018

British Library Cataloguing in Publication Data
Data available

ISBN: 978-0-19-276433-1

10 9 8 7 6 5 4 3 2 1

Paper used in the production of this book is a natural, recyclable product made from wood grown in sustainable forests. The manufacturing process conforms to the environmental regulations of the country of origin.

Printed in China

Acknowledgements

Series Editor: Annemarie Young

Additional artwork by Nick Schon

Tips for reading *A Lucky Find*

Children learn best when reading is relaxed and enjoyable.

- Talk about the title and the picture on page 6. Then read the speech bubble.

- Discuss what you think the story might be about.

- Encourage your child to read as much of the story as they can.

- Give lots of praise as your child reads, and help them when necessary.

- If your child gets stuck on a word that is decodable, encourage them to say the sounds and then blend them together to read the word. Read the whole sentence again. Focus on the meaning.

- If the word is not decodable, or is still too tricky, just read the word for them, re-read the sentence and move on.

- Where you can, use voices for different characters. Encourage your child to do the same. Reading with expression is fun.

- When you've finished reading the story, talk about it with your child, using the 'Talk about the story' questions at the end. Then do the activity.

Children enjoy re-reading stories, and this helps to build their confidence.

Have fun!

For more activities, free eBooks and practical advice to help your child progress with reading visit **oxfordowl.co.uk**

A Lucky Find

What do Kipper and Lee find on their walk?

It had rained all week. By Saturday the rain still hadn't stopped. Floppy looked miserable. He hadn't had a good walk for ages.

"Poor old Floppy," said Kipper.

Later that day, it stopped raining, so Kipper
opened the back door and looked out. He could see
a patch of blue sky.

"Good boy, Floppy," said Kipper. "It has stopped
raining at last."

Floppy picked up his lead in his mouth and gave
a little whimper.

"I'll see who will take you for a walk," said Kipper.

Biff and Chip were playing a game. It was hard
to tell who would win.

"Shall we take Floppy for a walk?" asked Kipper.

"Not just now," said Chip. "Biff and I are locked
in combat."

Mum and Dad were putting a bookcase together.

"Can we take Floppy for a walk?" pleaded Kipper. "He hasn't had one for ages."

"We can't," said Mum. "Not at the moment. Let him into the garden for now."

Just then, Kipper's friend Lee came to the door.

"Do you want to come to my house and play?" asked Lee. "Grandpa Chen has made some fortune cookies."

"Sorry, Floppy," said Kipper. "No walk for you at the moment."

The boys loved Grandpa's fortune cookies. Kipper broke one open and pulled out the tiny slip of paper from inside it. It said 'Kind deeds are like seeds. Plant them often'.

"I'd like to take Floppy for a walk," said Kipper. "That would be a kind deed."

"Well, Button needs a walk, too," said Lee. "Can we take both dogs out, Grandpa? That will be a kind deed."

Grandpa said it was a good idea.

"The dogs can have a good run," he said.

They went along a path that led to Dewdrop Down.
The boys loved going there and so did the dogs. It
had humps and bumps, and there were bushes to hide
behind. It was a great place to play chase.

Lee and Kipper ran up a steep hump. As they reached the top, the earth suddenly slid away. The boys tumbled to the bottom.

Grandpa Chen ran up to the boys. He helped them both up.

"Are you all right?" asked Grandpa.

"The ground gave way," said Lee. "We're just a bit muddy, that's all."

Kipper looked at the place where the ground had
slipped away. A black object was sticking out of
the earth.

"What is that, Grandpa Chen?" he asked.

"Oh, goodness!" exclaimed Grandpa Chen. "It might be dangerous. It looks like a very old explosive. It was probably dropped in World War Two."

"We'd better get well back," said Lee.

Grandpa Chen phoned the police. Soon, a police car raced up. Grandpa Chen took the police officers to the place where the ground had slipped away.

"It could be an explosive," said an officer.

"This is a job for the experts," said another officer. "Meanwhile, we must not take any chances. We'll have to tape off a large area."

The other police officer unrolled a large reel of blue tape.

It wasn't long before a disposal unit came. One of the experts went to look.

Lee and Kipper were excited.

"Wow!" said Lee. "Maybe we will see them explode it."

The disposal expert came to talk to the boys. He was grinning.

"It isn't a job for us after all," he said. "I think it's some kind of pot. But it's very old. It's an artefact and it needs a history expert."

The men went over the ground with metal detectors.

"There may be other artefacts under the ground," one of them said. "This could be an ancient village or burial ground."

Later, a woman called Anne came and carefully dug the pot out of the ground. She scraped some earth from the neck. Then she peered inside.

"This is so exciting," she said. "I'm hoping there is something interesting inside it."

Gently Anne tipped the pot up on to a cloth. About thirty gold coins slid out. Everyone gasped.

"These coins are hundreds of years old," she said, excitedly. "They show a Saxon king called Eadbald. He was king in about 620."

Kipper and Lee looked at one of the coins through a magnifying glass.

"I've never seen anything so old," said Lee.

"King Eadbald had a big nose," laughed Kipper, "and a big chin."

Then a television crew came.

"We'd like to cover the story on the news this evening," a man said. He looked at Lee and Kipper. "Now just tell us how you found the pot with all the gold coins in it."

Next, the crew spoke to Anne.

"The boys and their grandfather did the right thing," she said. "There may be more things to find. This could be the site of a Saxon village here on Dewdrop Down.

It is very exciting."

Back at home Chip rushed up to Kipper.

"Guess what?" he said. "I am the winner! I beat Biff but only just."

"Well, you should have come on the walk with us," said Kipper. "It was fantastic."

"We've finished the bookcase," said Dad.

"Did you have a nice walk?" asked Mum.

Kipper was bursting to tell everyone his news, but he didn't. "It was really interesting," he said. Then he turned on the television.

Everyone gasped when the news item came on. The reporter said that two boys had found a Saxon artefact.

Lee told the reporter how they had found it when the ground slipped away.

"I wish we'd gone on the walk now," said Biff.
"It would have been better than playing a silly old
computer game."

"Plant good deeds like seeds," said Kipper. "You'll
be amazed what they grow into."

"What are you talking about?" asked Biff.

There had been a Saxon village on Dewdrop Down.
The children went to see it. Anne was there to show
them round.

"It's an excavation," said Anne. "It means we find
where the village was by digging."

"It doesn't look much like a village," said Chip. "It's just a lot of pits and trenches."

"Saxon houses were made of wood," said Anne, "so there is nothing left of them. But we can tell where they stood."

"This is an exciting find," said Anne. "It's a gold band. It's a bit crumpled, but it has some Latin writing on it."

"It looks like one of Grandpa's fortune cookies," laughed Lee.

"It was thanks to the fortune cookies we took the dogs for a walk," Lee went on.

"Yes," said Kipper. "The fortune cookie was right, 'Kind deeds are like seeds. Plant them often'. We planted a good deed and it grew into finding a Saxon village."

"I've never made fortune cookies before," Grandpa laughed. "We didn't have them in Hong Kong when I grew up. They were invented in the USA."

"Well, keep making them," laughed Lee. "Your first ones were very lucky!"

Talk about the story

Why did the boys take the dogs for a walk?

Why did Grandpa Chen phone the police?

Why is there nothing left of Saxon houses?

What interesting things have you found on a walk?

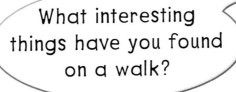

Odd one out

Here are nine ancient coins. Match up four pairs of coins and spot the odd one out.

Tips for reading *Egyptian Adventure*

Children learn best when reading is relaxed and enjoyable.

- Talk about the title and the picture on page 42. Then read the speech bubble.

- Discuss what you think the story might be about.

- Encourage your child to read as much of the story as they can.

- Give lots of praise as your child reads, and help them when necessary.

- If your child gets stuck on a word that is decodable, encourage them to say the sounds and then blend them together to read the word. Read the whole sentence again. Focus on the meaning.

- If the word is not decodable, or is still too tricky, just read the word for them, re-read the sentence and move on.

- Where you can, use voices for different characters. Encourage your child to do the same. Reading with expression is fun.

- When you've finished reading the story, talk about it with your child, using the 'Talk about the story' questions at the end. Then do the activity.

Children enjoy re-reading stories, and this helps to build their confidence.

Have fun!

For more activities, free eBooks and practical advice to help your child progress with reading visit **oxfordowl.co.uk**

Egyptian Adventure

What happens to Floppy and the children in Ancient Egypt?

Nadim and Anneena came to play at Biff and Chip's house. Nadim had a book about the Ancient Egyptians.

"It isn't just a book to read," said Nadim. "It's a special sort of book."

"It's a model book," said Nadim.

He opened it to show everyone.

"I get it," said Chip. "You press out the shapes. Then you fold and glue them to make a model."

The book had lots of shapes to press out and fold.
Nadim pointed to one.

"Can you see what this will be?" he asked.

"Of course we can," said Anneena. "It will be
a pyramid."

Chip found some glue. Then Nadim pressed out
the shapes and the others began to fold them. First
they made the pyramids. Anneena had a difficult
shape to fold.

"This is a sphinx," she said.

They pressed out some tiny trees and people. Biff
glued them all on to a sheet of paper. It made a scene
of Ancient Egypt. The children were pleased with it.

"I'm really pleased with the sphinx," said Anneena.

At last the model was finished. It looked so good
they called Mum upstairs to have a look.

"What a good job you made of it," said Mum. "I
like the pyramids and the sphinx."

"The sphinx was hard to make," said Anneena.

Floppy ran into the room. He didn't see the model
on the floor and he trod on it with his big paws. He
knocked over a tree and crushed the sphinx.

"Oh, Floppy!" everyone yelled.

Floppy looked unhappy. He knew he had upset the children.

"Never mind," said Chip. "It wasn't Floppy's fault. The sphinx looks even better than before."

Suddenly the magic key began to glow. The key
took the children back in time. It took Floppy too.

"It's not my day!" thought Floppy. "First, I get into
trouble. Now, it's a magic adventure."

The magic took them back to Ancient Egypt. They were standing by a pyramid. The pyramid was still being built. Far off they could see two more pyramids.

"This is amazing!" said Nadim. "I didn't think the pyramids were so big."

Some people were pulling on long ropes. They were moving a big block of stone.

"That's amazing too," said Chip. "I didn't know the pyramids were made with such big blocks of stone."

"Look over there!" gasped Anneena. She pointed to a huge stone sphinx. "Let's go and look at the sphinx," she said.

They all began to run towards it. Floppy didn't go with them. He had seen a cat!

The cat hissed at Floppy. Floppy couldn't stop himself. He chased it! It leaped on to some blocks of stone. Floppy jumped up too, but the cat was too fast for him.

Biff saw Floppy chase the cat. She called to the others. They all went back to get Floppy, but he was stuck on the blocks of stone. He couldn't get down.

"Oh Floppy! You silly dog," said Biff.

The children looked up at Floppy.

"He's a long way up!" laughed Nadim.

"I'll just have to climb up and help him down,"
said Biff.

Then a man ran over. He looked at Floppy
and gasped.

The man called to some people. They ran over to
the children. At first they were talking and shouting.
Then they all went quiet.

"What are they doing?" asked Biff. "Why are they
looking at us like this?"

The people put their hands together and raised them in the air. Then they sank down on their knees.

"They are bowing to us," said Chip. "They must think we're important."

"How strange!" said Nadim.

The people were not bowing down to the children. They were bowing to Floppy.

"I don't believe it!" whispered Chip. "They must think Floppy is important. I wonder why?"

The people took Floppy away. The children followed. Floppy couldn't believe all this was happening to him.

"A magic adventure is bad enough," he thought, "and now this!"

The people took Floppy to the king's palace. The king came out on to the steps.

"In Egypt a king is called a pharaoh," said Chip. "This pharaoh looks very fierce."

Everyone bowed when they saw him.

"We'd better bow down, too," said Biff. "We don't want to get into trouble."

A man spoke to the pharaoh.

"Great Pharaoh!" he said. "See what we have brought."

"The yellow dog!" gasped the pharaoh.

The pharaoh took Floppy inside the palace. Then he clapped his hands.

"Look after the yellow dog," he said. "Give him whatever he wants."

"Hmm!" thought Floppy. "I'm beginning to enjoy this adventure."

"I just don't get it," said Biff. "Why are they
making this fuss of Floppy?"

The pharaoh clapped his hands again. Some people
ran into the palace. One of them began to paint a
picture of Floppy.

Suddenly Biff sneezed. The pharaoh saw
the children.

"Strangers in my palace," he shouted. "How did
they get in?"

A guard grabbed Chip and Anneena. Another one
grabbed Biff and Nadim.

The guards took the children outside. They took
them to one of the pyramids. The people were moving
the big blocks of stone.

"You all look strong," said a guard. "You can
work here."

The children had to help pull one of the big blocks. They had to put rollers down to slide it along.

"This is hard work," moaned Biff. "These rollers are heavy."

It was time for a rest. The children had to drink from a skin bag.

"Ugh!" said Chip. "This water is warm and it tastes funny too. I'd rather have an ice-cold can."

The Egyptians were carving a giant stone block.
The children had to pick up all the chips of stone that
fell off.

"This is hard work, too," said Nadim.

"It's no fun being an Egyptian slave."

Anneena looked at the carving.

"I wonder if they are making a sphinx?" she said.
"A sphinx has the body of a lion but that doesn't look
like a lion's tail."

"Hmm! That tail looks familiar," said Biff.

The carving was finished.

"I said it looked familiar," gasped Biff. "It isn't a sphinx at all – it's Floppy."

At that moment the pharaoh came to see the carving. Some Egyptians carried Floppy.

Suddenly the magic key began to glow. Floppy
jumped down and ran over to the children.

"Come back, yellow dog," called the pharaoh.

"I'm glad it's time to go," thought Floppy. "It was
all getting too much of a good thing."

"What an adventure," said Nadim. "I didn't like being an Egyptian slave."

Anneena picked up the model sphinx.

"A sphinx has a lion's body and a man's head," she said. "But this does look a bit like Floppy."

Talk about the story

Why did the people bow down to Floppy?

How were the large blocks of stone moved to build the pyramid?

Why was Floppy glad it was time to go?

What would you like to build or make?

Who's who?

The Egyptian people come from Egypt. Test yourself on the name of the people who come from the following countries. The answers are upside down.

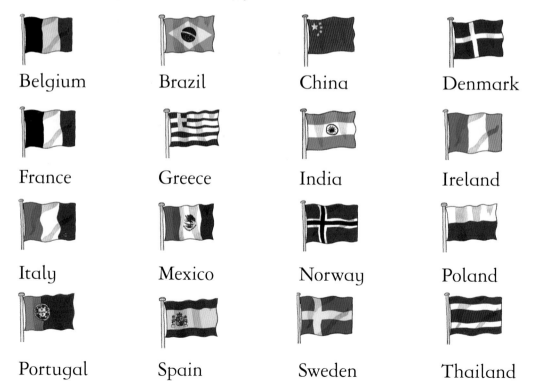

Belgium   Brazil   China   Denmark

France   Greece   India   Ireland

Italy   Mexico   Norway   Poland

Portugal   Spain   Sweden   Thailand

Belgian, Brazilian, Chinese, Danish / Danes, French, Greek, Indian, Irish, Italian, Mexican, Norwegian, Polish, Portuguese, Spanish, Swedish, Thai.

Tips for reading *The Travelling Players*

Children learn best when reading is relaxed and enjoyable.

- Talk about the title and the picture on page 78. Then read the speech bubble.

- Discuss what you think the story might be about.

- Encourage your child to read as much of the story as they can.

- Give lots of praise as your child reads, and help them when necessary.

- If your child gets stuck on a word that is decodable, encourage them to say the sounds and then blend them together to read the word. Read the whole sentence again. Focus on the meaning.

- If the word is not decodable, or is still too tricky, just read the word for them, re-read the sentence and move on.

- Where you can, use voices for different characters. Encourage your child to do the same. Reading with expression is fun.

- When you've finished reading the story, talk about it with your child, using the 'Talk about the story' questions at the end. Then do the activity.

Children enjoy re-reading stories, and this helps to build their confidence.

Have fun!

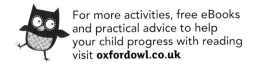

For more activities, free eBooks and practical advice to help your child progress with reading visit **oxfordowl.co.uk**

The Travelling Players

How do the children help the travelling players?

The children were putting on a play.

Wilf loved acting. "I'd like to be an actor one day," he said.

Chip was not so keen. "I can never remember my lines," he said.

"That's why I haven't given you a part," laughed Wilf.

Wilf was directing the play.

"It's a medieval play," he said. "People performed plays like this hundreds of years ago. Plays like this were performed by travelling players."

The play was about George and the dragon.
Wilf was George and Nadim was the dragon.

Nadim made flames shoot out of the dragon's
nostrils. He used a fan that blew red cloth but, so far,
only one nostril was working.

Chip didn't have a part. He had to prompt the
actors when they couldn't remember their lines.

"The prompter is very important," said Wilf.

But Chip was bored. He ran upstairs and went into
Biff's room to borrow her charger for his game.

Wilma began to say her lines, "*Here come I, a mighty knight . . .*" when Dad came in.

"Sorry, everyone," said Dad. "I have to hoover the carpet. Would you mind going somewhere else?"

"Let's practise our lines in my room," said Biff.

In Biff's room, Chip saw the key lying on the floor. He picked it up and suddenly it began to glow.

"Oh no!" said Chip. "Not another adventure! I'm all by myself as well! And just when I was about to go up a level on my game."

At that moment, the rest of the children came
upstairs. Just as the key began to glow, they walked
into Biff's room. It whisked them all into the adventure
as well.

The key took Chip to a wood. There was no sign of the others. Then he heard two men coming through the wood towards him. They were talking loudly.

Quickly, Chip crouched down behind a bush so that he couldn't be seen.

Chip heard one of the men say, "She's worked hard to gain their trust. She knows what to do. We can't let the Essex lot win again."

Chip wondered what this strange conversation meant. He sank lower in the bush, but as he did so a twig snapped.

One of the men spun round. "Who's spying on us?"
he yelled. He ran towards the bush waving a stick.

Chip gasped. His heart pounded. He jumped out
and ran off as fast as he could.

The other man laughed. "It's just a boy," he said.

Meanwhile, the other children arrived in the adventure but in a different place. They were on a road. Lying in the middle of it was a helmet. Further on were a dish and a gold crown.

"Strange!" said Nadim. "Why has somebody dropped all these things in the road?"

The children hurried on. Round the corner was a
large wagon. On the back, a chest had fallen over.
The lid was open and things were dropping out.

The wagon lurched into a rut and the dragon
slipped sideways.

"Mind the dragon," a woman shouted. "It's our most expensive prop."

"I think the key has brought us back to the Middle Ages," said Anneena. "These people are travelling actors."

Wilma gave the props back to the woman.

"Oh, thank you," said the woman. "We need these things. We are 'The Essex Players'."

"We're going to Saint Albans," a man added. "Other groups of actors will be there. We are all taking part in a competition for the Mayor's Purse. The best play wins a purse of silver."

"We are actors, too," said Wilf. "Our play is about George and the dragon."

"Well, I doubt if you could win the competition," said the woman. "We have won it every year for the past three years. Besides, you are too young."

The children walked with the Essex Players, but it was slow with the heavy wagon.

"The wagon is our stage," explained the woman, whose name was Beth. "It carries all we need."

At last the players stopped to eat some food.

One of the players did not sit and eat with the
others. She sat on a tree stump sewing a costume.

"Come and eat with us, Jan," an actor called.

"No, I need to work on the costumes," said Jan.

"She's a new member of our company," said Beth.
"She looks after the costumes."

Just then, Chip arrived. He looked really pleased to see them.

"I'm so glad you're in the adventure too!" he panted. "I thought I was all alone."

"These are travelling players," said Wilf. "They are taking part in the competition at St Albans."

Chip glanced at Jan. What was she sprinkling into one of the costumes? He remembered the conversation he had heard earlier on between the two men. But he wasn't sure if it had anything to do with Jan.

Soon they reached St Albans. The town was full of actors getting ready for the competition.

"I'm glad we've got here," said Nadim. "The dragon's head *was* getting heavy."

The Essex Players set up their wagon and put on their costumes.

"The wagons are set round the market square," said Beth. "Each company acts in turn. We're on first."

"Where's Jan?" asked an actor. "She needs to check our costumes."

Suddenly Beth began to scratch herself.

Then all the actors began to scratch. One of them pulled off his shirt and another began to hop and rub his skin.

"We can't perform like this," said one. "Someone has put something in our costumes to make us itch. It's to stop us putting on our play."

"Ooh! Aaah!" gasped Beth, scratching herself all over. "The play is due to start any minute. There's only one thing for it. You children must put on *your* play instead."

Wilf gulped. "We'll do it," he said. "If we can do it here, we can do it anywhere."

There was no time to feel nervous. A crowd had
gathered in front of the wagon.

"Where's Chip?" hissed Nadim. "He's not here."

Wilf climbed on to the stage and stepped forward.
"We are 'The Young Essex Players'," he announced.
"We present 'George and the Dragon'."

The people laughed. "Children! They can't act,"
a man bellowed.

"That does it!" said Wilma. "We'll show them!
*Here come I, a mighty knight. I come from lands afar to
fight.*" She swung her sword just as someone threw
an apple.

Wilma's sword hit the apple. Splat! It broke into fragments showering the crowd.

"What a shot!" yelled someone.

After that, the play went well. The crowd cheered when Nadim's dragon came on breathing fire.

    As the play ended, Chip came on to the stage with
the Mayor. The Mayor held Jan by the arm.

    "Tell the people what you did," the Mayor demanded.
"Tell them what you put in the players' costumes."

    "It was itching powder," said Jan sadly.

"The Oxford Actors paid me to do it. They
gave me the itching powder. They want to win the
competition," sniffed Jan.

The crowd booed and hissed.

"The Oxford Actors are banned from the contest,"
the Mayor announced. "Arrest this woman. Find
the Oxford Actors and drive them out of town."

The Mayor went on, "The competition will be postponed until the itching powder has worn off. Here's a small reward for acting so well and for catching a cheat." He gave a small bag of silver coins to Chip.

"I'm glad you weren't in the play," said Wilf. "It meant you could catch Jan before she got away."

"We will never know if the Essex Players will win the competition," said Chip. "The key is glowing."

The children put on their play in the garden.

Chip sat in the audience. "I've checked the costumes for itching powder," he laughed to himself. "And they don't need me to prompt them."

"The Young Essex Players present 'George and the Dragon'," announced Wilf.

At the end, the players gave a bow.

"They were good," said Nadim's dad. "You would think they had done it all before."

"He doesn't know that they have," thought Chip. "Thanks to itching powder."

Talk about the story

What prize do the travelling players expect to win?

What was the plot? Did it work?

What made the audience change their minds about the children's acting?

What part would you like to play in a film or a story?

What is it?

In the story, itching powder is used which makes the players twitch and scratch.

The following pictures show eight things that end in *-tch*. What are the words?

watch, witch, stitch, catch, hutch, thatch, patch, crutch

Tips for reading *The Flying Machine*

Children learn best when reading is relaxed and enjoyable.

- Talk about the title and the picture on page 114. Then read the speech bubble.

- Discuss what you think the story might be about.

- Encourage your child to read as much of the story as they can.

- Give lots of praise as your child reads, and help them when necessary.

- If your child gets stuck on a word that is decodable, encourage them to say the sounds and then blend them together to read the word. Read the whole sentence again. Focus on the meaning.

- If the word is not decodable, or is still too tricky, just read the word for them, re-read the sentence and move on.

- Where you can, use voices for different characters. Encourage your child to do the same. Reading with expression is fun.

- When you've finished reading the story, talk about it with your child, using the 'Talk about the story' questions at the end. Then do the activity.

Children enjoy re-reading stories, and this helps to build their confidence.

Have fun!

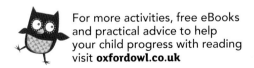

For more activities, free eBooks and practical advice to help your child progress with reading visit **oxfordowl.co.uk**

The Flying Machine

What happens to the two young inventors' flying machine?

Nadim was at the airport with his mum and dad.
They had been to America for a holiday. Now it was
time to fly home.

Nadim's dad was nervous.

"I don't like flying," he said. "I hate taking off."

"I don't hate it," said Nadim. "I love it."

On the flight there was a surprise for Nadim. The steward asked him if he wanted to see the controls.

Nadim was excited. He had always wanted to see the flight deck of an aeroplane.

"Oh brilliant!" he said. "Yes, please!"

The steward took Nadim and his dad through the
aeroplane.

"These planes are huge," said Nadim.

"They hold about four hundred people," said
the steward.

"That's a lot of people in one plane," said Nadim.

Nadim and his dad went on to the flight deck. They met the captain.

"We're flying on auto-pilot," said the captain. "The plane is flying by itself."

Nadim looked at all the controls.

"I'd like to be a pilot," he said.

"It takes a long time to learn," said the Captain.
"But what's to stop you?"

"Don't let him take over the controls just yet," joked
Nadim's dad. "I'm a nervous passenger."

"Oh Dad!" said Nadim.

After Nadim got home, he went to play at Biff and Chip's house.

Anneena was already there.

Nadim told everyone about his holiday.

"I went on to the flight deck of the aeroplane," he said.

"I'd love to be a pilot," said Anneena.

Mum called Biff and Chip. They had to go
downstairs to help wash up.

"We won't be long," said Chip.

Anneena picked up the magic key. Suddenly it began
to glow. It took Anneena and Nadim on an adventure.

The magic took Nadim and Anneena back in time.
It took them to a place in America.

"Why has the magic key brought us here?" asked
Anneena.

They heard the sound of an engine. The sound was
coming out of a big cloud of dust.

A man was driving towards them in a strange-looking car.

"What on earth is it?" asked Nadim. "It looks like a really old car."

"You can't stand there!" called the man. "You'll be in the way of the flying machine."

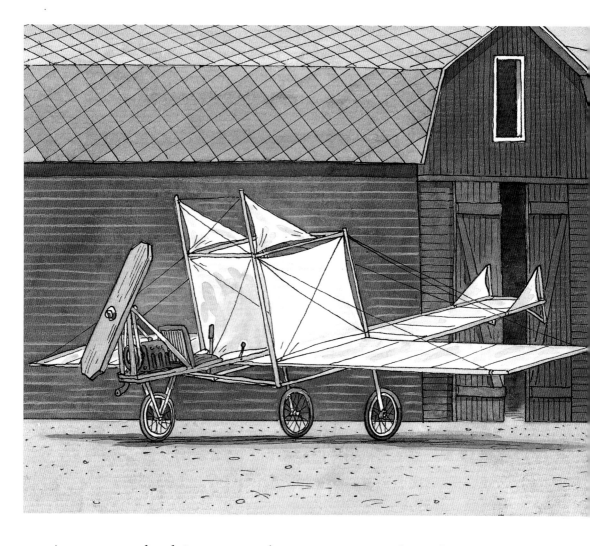

A strange-looking aeroplane was standing by a barn. Nadim and Anneena had never seen anything like it.

Another man was working on the aeroplane. The first man got out of the car and went over to him.

Anneena gasped. The two men looked alike.

"They must be twins," she said to Nadim.

"Hello," said the second man. "I'm Henry and this is my twin brother, Harold. Who are you?"

"I'm Nadim. This is Anneena," said Nadim.

"You're not spying on us, are you?" asked Harold.

"Why would we do that?" asked Anneena.

"We're just about to try out the flying machine," said Henry, "but it's a secret."

"No one has ever made a flying machine before," said Harold. "We will be the first people to do it."

"It's amazing," said Nadim. "We've not seen an aeroplane like this before."

The twins laughed. "A hairy plane," said Harold. "That's a good name for it – a hairy plane!"

"But it will never fly," said Anneena.

"Of course it will," said Henry.

Harold sat in the flying machine.

"I'm ready!" he shouted.

Henry started the engine.

The propeller began to turn. It spun faster and faster. But the flying machine didn't move.

"I told you so," said Anneena.

"It's the propeller," said Anneena. "It will never work. It's too flat."

She picked up two pieces of wood.

"It needs to be like this," she said. "It acts like a screw to pull the plane through the air."

"Well, we could try it," said Henry.

The twins changed the shape of the propeller.

"But it still won't fly," said Nadim. "You only have a flat wing. You have no way to make it lift up. How will it take off?"

"Ha!" said Harold. "We've made a ramp! The faster we go, the higher it will fly."

Harold got into the aeroplane. Henry started the engine.

"We'll see if you're right," he yelled.

The propeller spun round and the aeroplane began to move faster and faster.

"It's working!" shouted Henry.

"It still won't fly," said Nadim.

The plane zoomed up the ramp at full speed. It rose in the air like a heavy bird.

"Yee-ha!" called Henry. "It's flying."

The plane flew straight up. It went backwards in a loop. Then it dived towards the ground.

"Help!" yelled Harold.

The plane hit the ground with a heavy bump.
Harold was thrown out.

It was still going at full speed. It roared towards
Nadim and Anneena.

"Stop it!" yelled Harold.

"Look out!" shouted Henry.

No one could stop the plane. It headed towards a big water tank.

"It's going to crash!" gasped Nadim.

The plane went under the water tank. The wings snapped off, but the plane went on.

"It hasn't stopped," said Henry.

The plane didn't slow down. It roared on towards
a farm.

Harold and Henry jumped into their car and chased
after it.

"One thing's for sure," said Nadim to Anneena,
"your propeller works well."

Henry and Harold's mother and father lived on the farm. Their mother had just done the washing. She was hanging it out to dry. Their father was watering his prize melons and pumpkins.

Henry and Harold followed. Nadim and Anneena
chased after them.

"Aw heck!" said Harold. "Why won't it stop?"

"Oh my!" said Henry. "It's heading for the farm."

"Oh dear," said Anneena. "I don't like the look
of this."

The plane roared on. It ran through the washing. It squashed the melons and pumpkins.

"It hasn't stopped," shouted Harold. "Now what are we going to do?"

"Let's hope it runs out of gas soon," said Henry.

The plane headed towards the town. A woman was painting her house. She heard the sound of an engine.

"Whatever is that?" she wondered. "It sounds like a roaring bull."

The plane ran into the ladder and knocked it down.

The woman fell to the ground. She still had the paint brush in her hand.

The plane went on.

"What the heck was that?" gasped the woman.

At last the plane stopped in the middle of the town. It had crashed into a statue.

People ran to see what all the noise was about.

Henry and Harold stopped the car. They both jumped out.

"This doesn't look good," said Harold.

Nadim and Anneena ran to see where the plane had
stopped.

Nadim spoke to Harold and Henry.

"You see!" he said. "The propeller works. Now you
need to make flaps and a rudder."

Suddenly there was a noise. It sounded like an engine. It came from up in the sky.

Everyone looked up. An aeroplane was flying over the town.

"It's a flying machine!" someone shouted.

"Another hairy plane," joked Anneena.

The people waved and cheered. The pilot of the plane waved back at them.

"I know who that is," called a man. "It's Wilbur Wright. He and his brother are the first men to fly."

"Well I'll be darned!" said Henry.

"So we aren't the first men to fly after all," said Henry. "The Wright brothers have beaten us to it."

"Never mind," said Harold. "I have an idea for a boat that goes under the water."

The magic key began to glow. It was time for Nadim and Anneena to go.

"Sorry we were such a long time," said Biff. "There was a lot of washing up to do."

"Never mind," laughed Anneena. "The time just flew by."

"And it wasn't just the time that flew," joked Nadim.

Talk about the story

What did Anneena suggest to make the propeller work?

What suggestions did Nadim make after the plane still wouldn't fly?

What was the twins' next idea? Do you think they succeeded?

What would you like to invent?

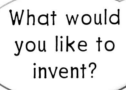

Word twins

We often hear words that go together to make an expression such as 'huff and puff' or 'pins and needles'. These are called word twins. Match the following words to make word twins.

loud and …	bustle
heads or …	clear
cops and …	thin
hustle and …	white
sink or …	tat
tit for …	tails
black and …	robbers
thick or …	swim

Remembering the stories together

Encourage your child to remember and retell the stories in this book. You could ask questions like these:

- Who are the characters?
- What happens at the beginning?
- What happens next?
- How does the story end?
- What was your favourite part? Why?

Story prompts

When talking to your child about the stories, you could use these more detailed reminders to help them remember the exact sequence of events. Turn the statements below into questions, so that your child can give you the answers. For example, *Who takes Floppy for a walk? What do they find?* And so on …

A Lucky Find

- Kipper and Lee take Floppy for a walk.
- They discover something buried in the mud and call the police in case it is dangerous.
- It turns out to be an old pot full of very old coins.
- The boys are interviewed for a TV programme.

Egyptian Adventure

- The key takes the children back to ancient Egypt.
- The people are amazed to see a yellow dog. So is the Pharaoh.
- The guards put the children to work and they help make an enormous carving.
- It turns out to be an enormous Floppy instead of a sphinx!

The Travelling Players

- The children are putting on a medieval play when the magic key takes them back in time.

- Chip overhears a plot to cheat in a competition.

- He finds the others who are with another group of actors. He suspects the costume lady.

- When the competition is about to start, some of the actors start itching, so they can't perform.

- The children have to put on their play instead. The guilty woman is taken away by the mayor.

- The magic key takes them home and the children put on their play again.

The Flying Machine

- Nadim and Anneena are taken on an adventure without the others.

- They meet some men who are working on creating a flying machine.

- Anneena advises them on how to make the propellor work.

- The plane runs out of control and crashes into everything in its path.

- It stops in the middle of town.

- They hear something in the sky and it's a flying machine! Someone else has made it work before them.

You could now encourage your child to create a 'story map' of each story, drawing and colouring all the key parts of them. This will help them to identify the main elements of the stories and learn to create their own stories.

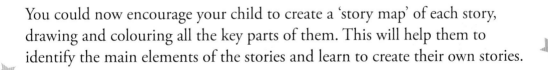